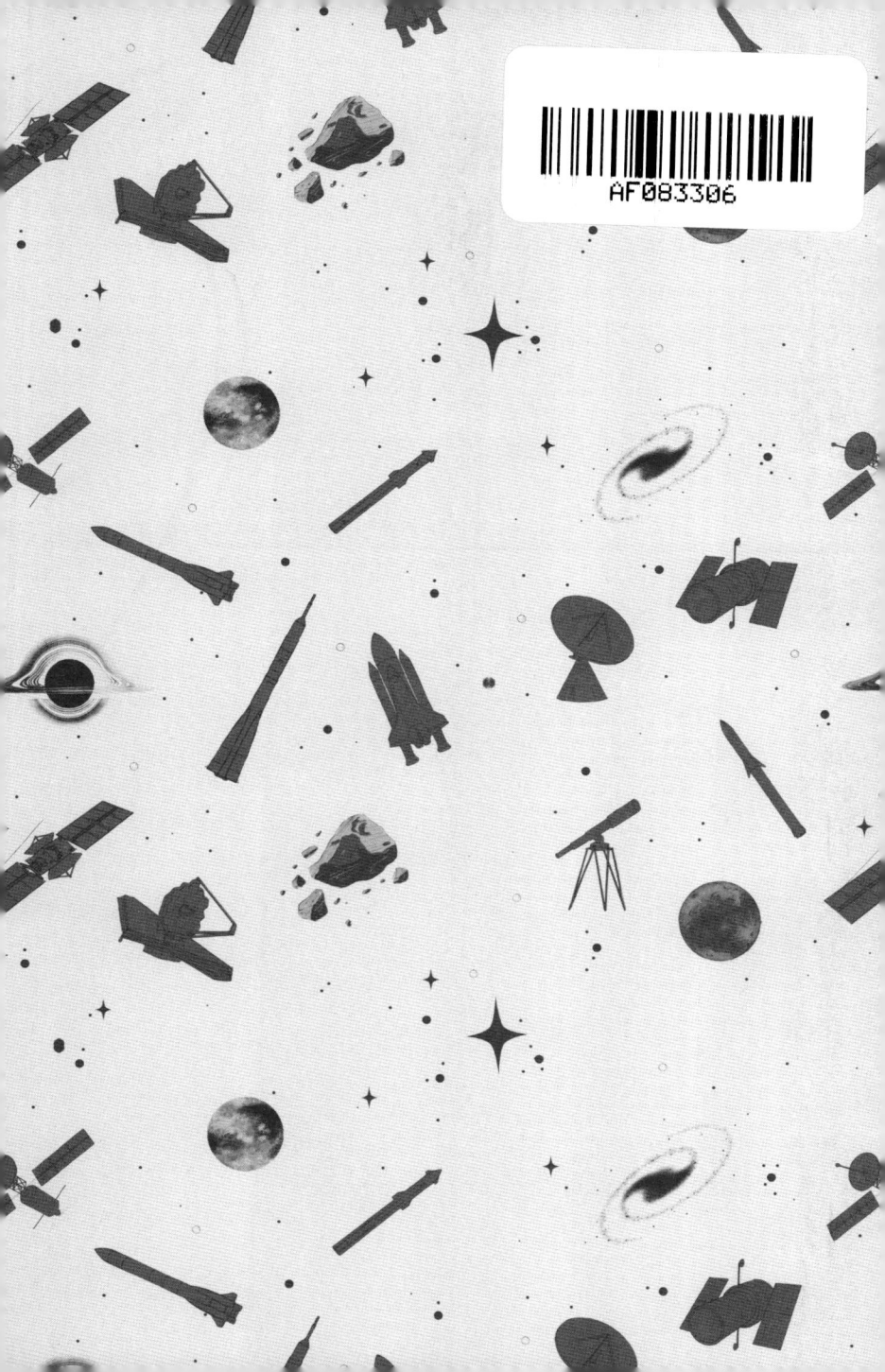

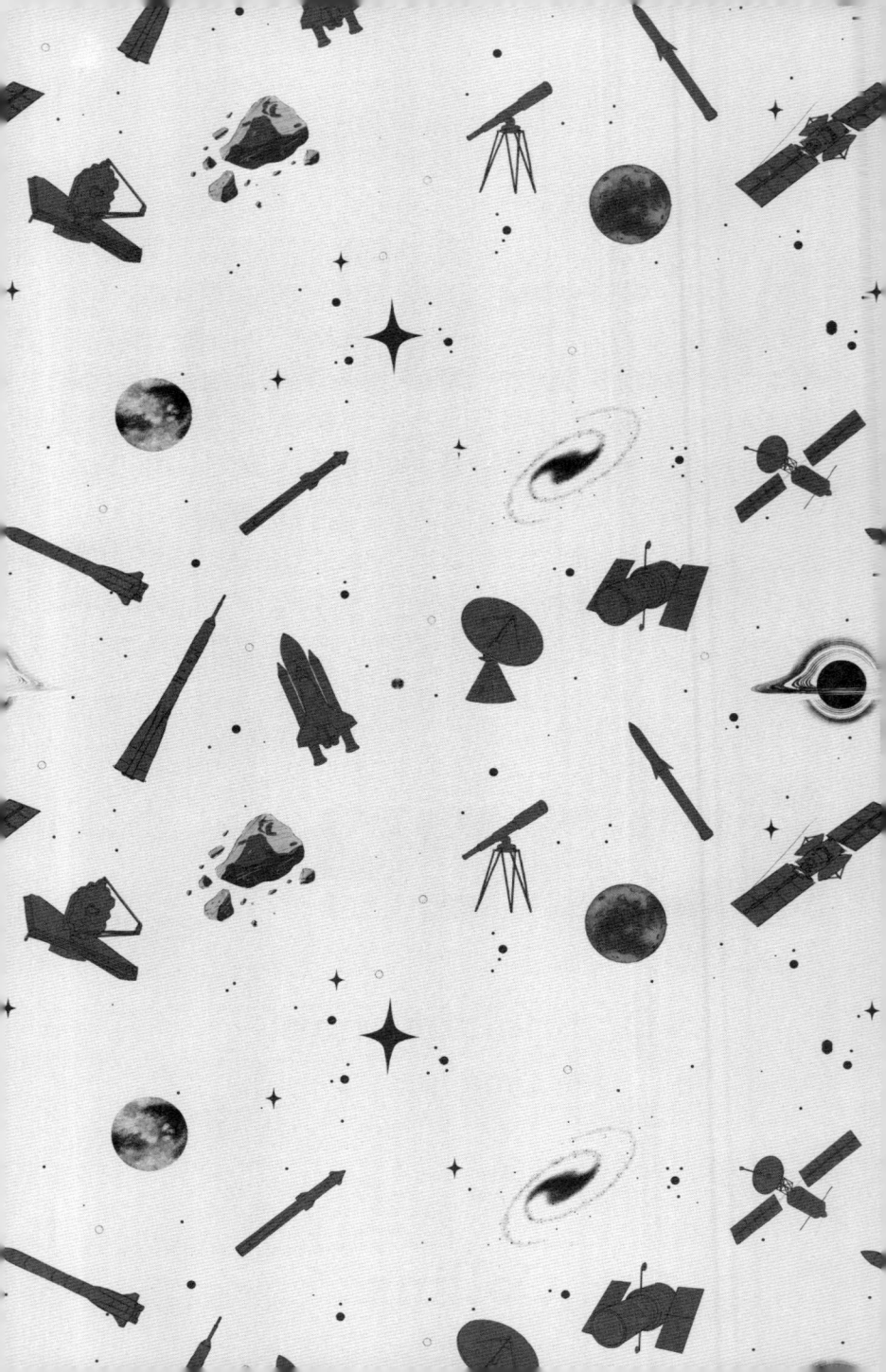

Mission: Space

Dr Sheila Kanani

Illustrated by Fifa Adoglo

Collins

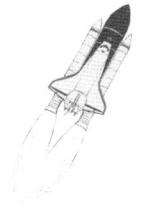

1. Look up!

When you look up at the night sky, what do you see? How does it make you feel? If it's a clear night, you might be able to see the Moon and the stars. But sometimes those tiny specks of light might be satellites, or meteors, or even the International Space Station (ISS) circling Earth.

People have always looked up and wondered if we're alone in the universe and if there might be life on other planets. It's big questions like these that have inspired humans to explore space. Humans are curious. People want to discover more about where they live, how Earth was made, and our place in the universe.

By studying our solar system, galaxy and the universe, we can try to work out where we came from, and what might happen to it all in the future.

Would you like to go into space? I would! I'm a planetary scientist and space educator and I've been fascinated by how our universe works for as long as I can remember. When I ask students what their top job might be in the space industry, one of the most popular answers is "astronaut". Being an astronaut might seem exciting and adventurous but it's a very challenging job (I'd still jump at the chance, though) and that's part of what makes it so extraordinary.

Astronauts do years of training before they go into space, and then they might spend six months on the ISS living in **microgravity**. They need to get used to floating around and sleeping in specially designed sleeping bags that can be secured to any large surface – even the ceiling! While on board, the astronauts carry out science experiments and communicate with people on Earth. They also make sure that the spacecraft is in good condition, by keeping it clean and making repairs.

The ISS in orbit above Earth.

There are lots of challenges to living in space, but it would still be amazing, wouldn't it? Imagine seeing Earth looking like a huge blue and green marble "floating" in the blackness. The ISS orbits Earth every 90 minutes which means the astronauts will see 16 sunrises and 16 sunsets every 24 hours. Spacewalks – when astronauts leave the space station and work outside – must also be an incredible experience.

Of course, there are physical and mental challenges. The astronauts are a support system for each other and work together to try to fix problems that come up. There are up to seven astronauts living and working on the ISS at one time, and they might be from different countries. It's important that they can work as a team, think logically and stay calm under pressure.

Astronauts must be very fit, and training doesn't stop when they're in space. They have to do about two hours of exercise every day to stop them losing strength in their bones and muscles brought on by the lack of gravity. There's a gym on the ISS with a treadmill, a stationary bicycle and special lifting weights. Even then, when they return to Earth, it might take from three to six months for astronauts' muscles to recover from being in space. It can take years for their bones to recover!

What about food? In the 1960s, the kind of food the very first astronauts ate was freeze-dried. Meals were prepared before the flight, frozen and then all the water was removed using a vacuum pump. Once they were in space, the astronauts rehydrated the food by adding water. Space food is a bit different to food on Earth – you can't just take a loaf of bread into space for sandwiches because the crumbs would float around and could damage the equipment.

Today, food is still freeze-dried but there are other options, too. On the ISS, there's a little kitchen so that food can be stored in a fridge and heated up, and the astronauts even have fresh fruit and vegetables delivered to them by automated spacecraft.

Even though it might be the first job we all think of, astronauts only make up a small part of the space industry. Space starts between 80 and 100 kilometres up from Earth's surface and getting there isn't easy. To get into space, you need to escape Earth's gravity using a powerful rocket. These rockets take off at speeds of more than 11 kilometers per second and sending just one person into space is the work of hundreds of people: engineers to build spacecraft and satellites, scientists to analyse the data, medical doctors to monitor the health of the astronauts, and communicators to tell people what has been found.

There are also lots of creative, art-based roles offered by places like the European Space Agency (ESA) and the National Aeronautics and Space Administration (NASA). Photographers and **videographers** record space projects carried out on Earth. The information is used as reference for future projects and made into short films to educate people. Designers make spacesuits, create mission logos, and even plan out areas for astronauts to live on the Moon.

An artist's design showing what living on other planets might look like in the future.

Space artists use information we have already discovered to imagine what new planets, spaceships, and **extraterrestrial** life forms might look like.

There are also jobs in space law, business, and communication – people with these skills help organise space missions and share discoveries with the world.

You don't have to work for a space agency to have a space-related creative career. Writers and storytellers create books and films about space adventures; game developers create immersive and interactive games set in space. What you see in an immersive game today might become reality in the future with hundreds of **space tourists** exploring the universe. So, if you love space but aren't as excited about science as I am, there might still be a place for you in a space-related job!

Today, there are more British women astronauts than there have ever been in the UK, and the number of women in space-related careers is growing. The ESA and NASA work with schools and other organisations to encourage more people to study STEM subjects: Science, Technology, Engineering and Maths. Without experts in STEM subjects, there would be no space industry. Now, there are girls all over the world planning their future in the space industry.

In the very early days of space exploration, most of the people working in the space industry and *all* of the astronauts were men. Throughout history, women working in the space industry have been forgotten or perhaps ignored. Sometimes they've had barriers to overcome, and maybe they weren't offered the same chances as men trying to get to the same position. It can be tricky to be the first person who does something different. It's much easier to aspire to do something if you can see someone who looks like you already doing well in that area.

Let's go back in time and see just how things were done in the early years of space exploration – before the ISS had been built, before modern technology made it quicker and easier to reach outer space – when women proved they could do the job just as well as men.

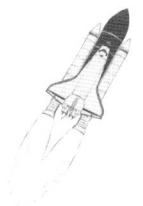

2. Valentina Tereshkova: First woman in space

Why was Valentina Tereshkova selected as the first woman from the **Soviet Union** to go into space? She wasn't a pilot or a scientist, she wasn't in the army, and she didn't work in the space industry. In fact, Valentina was from a small, rural village called Maslennikovo. She left school at 16 and worked in the same local textile factory as her mother while studying in the evening. Valentina had something every cosmonaut (the Russian word for astronaut) needed at that time: expertise in parachuting and skydiving.

The Yaroslav Sports Club wasn't far from where Valentina lived and she got into a new hobby – parachute jumping!

In 1959, when she was 22, Valentina completed her first parachute jump. She trained almost every weekend and completed night jumps over land and water. Sometimes, she would wait and wait before pulling the handle to open her parachute, just so she could feel the air as she returned to Earth. By 1961, when she was 24, she had completed over 100 jumps and become a competitive parachutist and skydiver. But why was this skill so important for cosmonauts?

Scientists and engineers in the Soviet space industry had created the technology to send cosmonauts into space. But after their mission, these cosmonauts didn't fly the space capsule home and land it gently on Earth. The capsules travelled at speed, and they weren't designed to land with a pilot inside. The only way for cosmonauts to get home was to jump out of the capsule with a parachute and land separately from the spacecraft. This wasn't just any jump – they had to eject from the capsule 7,000 metres above Earth! If they wanted to get back home safely, they had to know *how* to make this jump.

In the early 1960s, the Soviet Union and the US were competing to lead the way in space technology. The Soviets won the race when they sent Yuri Gagarin into space. Gagarin was the first person to complete a spaceflight, on 12th April 1961. The Soviet Union were ahead, and they wanted things to stay that way, so Nikolai Kamanin was put in charge of recruiting and training female cosmonauts. If the first woman in space was from the Soviet Union, they would beat the Americans to it for a second time!

The cosmonaut training programme started accepting applications from women, and more than 400 applied. By February 1962, five women were approved to be trained – and one of them was Valentina. This didn't mean she would automatically get to go into space. At the start of the training, only two of the five women were going to take a spaceflight, but which ones? First, the trainees had to learn about space, science, engineering, astronomy and … how to fly a space rocket!

The trainees were tested physically too. They had to be able to cope with the demands of space travel, like extreme temperatures and isolation. Physical tests included being spun around on a large, flattened metal sphere called a **centrifuge**. As the sphere rotated faster and faster, the trainees experienced what it would feel like during a rocket launch.

The training must have been tough! These women didn't come from military backgrounds and had to learn everything. They were taught about rockets, space, science, engineering, astronomy and so much more. They were tested physically to make sure they could withstand the demands of launching into space. This included being squashed in **decompression chambers** and put in rooms heated to over 70 degrees Celsius! They also experienced the feeling of weightlessness in a specially modified aeroplane and were isolated for ten days at a time. That's a lot! That must have meant they were nearly ready – right? No! As well as these simulations, they were also taught how to fly planes and swim in extreme conditions. After a year and a half of training, the five women learnt that only one of them would be going into space, not two. Valentina was the one chosen.

On 16th June 1963, Valentina travelled by bus to her spacecraft, a rocket called Vostok 6, which was sitting on the launch pad. Valentina was wearing a heavy, orange-coloured spacesuit and helmet and she sat alone in the capsule.

The countdown took two hours. Then, with a roar, the rocket blasted up into the sky and in minutes, Valentina was in space. Vostok 6 was in orbit and Valentina was gazing down at Earth! She had been given a call sign – a unique name to identify herself when she spoke to the team back on Earth – and hers was "Chaika", which means "seagull". Valentina sent a message back to Earth: "It is I, Seagull! Everything is fine. I see the horizon. A light blue, a beautiful band. This is the Earth. How beautiful it is! All goes well."

Valentina wasn't quite alone. There was already another Soviet ship in space, Vostok 5, piloted by Valery Bykovsky. As Valentina and Valery orbited Earth, their individual spacecraft got close enough for them to communicate by radio. There were also cameras inside Valentina's spacecraft – these sent live footage of her back to Earth, where the images were broadcast directly onto TV. Valentina had been told not to tell anyone about her cosmonaut training. Her mother only discovered the truth when she saw her daughter in space on her neighbour's TV! Valentina had told her she was at a parachuting competition.

Valentina's ship orbited Earth 48 times. She took photographs and wrote a flight log, where she recorded how her body felt, and communicated her discoveries with **mission control**. The photographs Valentina took of the horizon were later used to work out the different layers of Earth's atmosphere.

The mission lasted almost three days. The food made Valentina unwell, she suffered from space sickness, and she had to use a very **primitive** toilet. Valentina had toothpaste, but no one had packed a toothbrush for her. There were also problems with the capsule controls, which didn't work properly. Despite this, Valentina continued to record important information. The team back on Earth now had medical studies on the effect of spaceflight on both men *and* women.

Valentina in Vostok 6

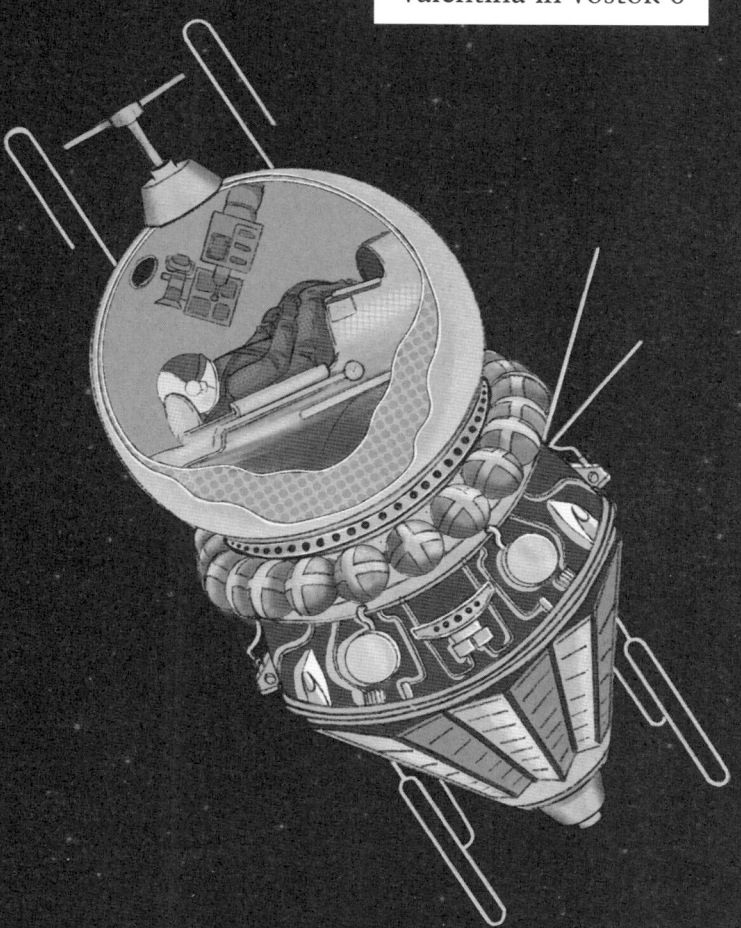

After nearly 71 hours in space, it was time to go home. But Valentina discovered that she had a bigger problem: the capsule was programmed to go up but not come down. Valentina alerted **ground control** and they had to send instructions via radio for her to reprogramme the capsule. Without reprogramming, Valentina would have travelled further into space and never returned to Earth.

She did it! Vostock 6 changed course and began to fall towards the ground. Valentina ejected from the capsule and opened her parachute. It was windy as she fell back to Earth, but all her training paid off. She bumped her nose on the edge of her helmet, but touchdown was a success. Valentina landed in Kazakhstan on 19th June 1963 and became an instant national hero. She was awarded medals and invited to speak to world leaders in many different countries. Later, a crater on the Moon was named "Tereshkova" after her, along with an asteroid called "Chaika" after Valentina's call sign.

Valentina never went into space again, even though she qualified to join a new group of female cosmonauts. She did travel widely for official visits and talked about women's education and the challenges women faced. She also studied space engineering at the Zhukovsky Air Force Engineering Academy and helped to train other cosmonauts and astronauts at the Yuri Gagarin Cosmonaut Training Centre – although it wasn't until 1982 that another Soviet woman, Svetlana Savitskaya, would go into space. In 1966, Valentina became a member of the World Peace Council.

Valentina still holds the record as the youngest woman to go into space – she was just 26. She is also the only woman to have completed a solo space mission.

If there's a seat on a ship travelling to Mars, Valentina has said she would like to be on it – even if it's a one-way trip. That might still be possible. Who knows?

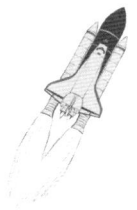

3. Dr Sally Ride: Youngest American astronaut

Sally Ride was the first American woman to fly into space, and the third woman after Valentina Tereshkova and Svetlana Savitskaya. Sally was interested in science when she was young, and her parents bought her a telescope and a chemistry set, but she was also sporty. She was accepted to an elite school for girls on a tennis scholarship, and she might have become a professional tennis player. When a teacher encouraged Sally to study the sciences, the course of her life changed.

After she finished school, Sally studied English and Physics at university. She went on to study Astrophysics and X-ray Astronomy, where she learnt about the physical nature of stars and the energy made by natural objects in space such as planets or asteroids. Not everyone who applies to the space programme has studied these courses, but when Sally spotted an advert in the paper saying that NASA was looking for new astronauts to fly the Space Shuttle, she thought she might have the skills they were looking for.

It was January 1977. At that time there had been no US female astronauts and most of the men training to be astronauts had come from a military background. This time, NASA had widened their search to include engineers and scientists – and women were able to apply for the first time. Sally was one of 8,000 people who applied! By January 1978, she was one of the final 35 astronaut candidates: 29 men and 6 women.

Astronaut candidates *aren't* astronauts yet. Like Valentina, Sally still had to undergo all the training to become an astronaut – and even then, she might not have been chosen to go into space.

She learnt how to survive in emergency situations, and trained to get in and out of a "rescue ball". The ball was made of layers of special fabric, and it was designed to transport a single astronaut from one space shuttle to another. She was instructed on how to fix broken equipment in extreme conditions, cope with weightlessness, fly a jet, and work the radio communications and navigation equipment.

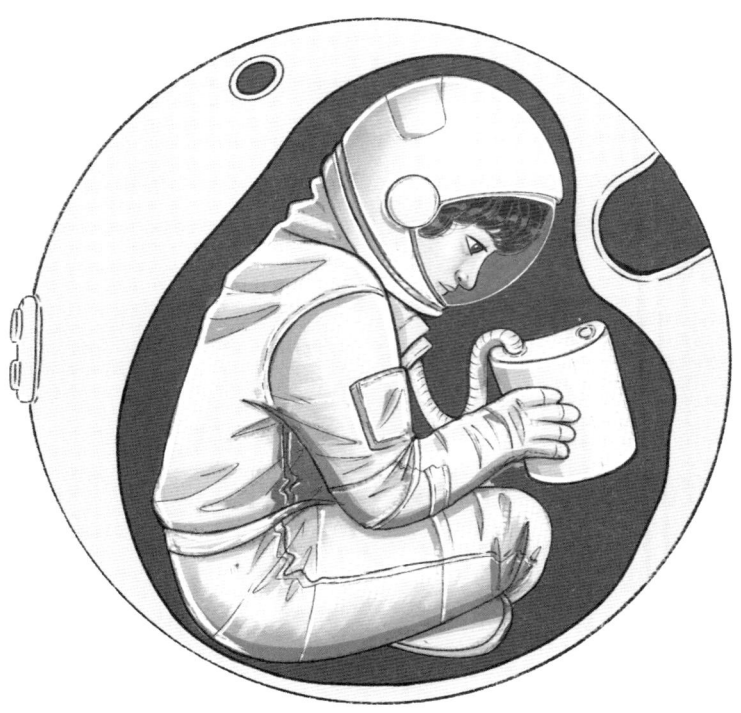

Sally also had to learn how to parachute jump, but not for the same reason as Valentina. No US astronaut has ever had to jump out of a return capsule. So, how do they get home?

The US designed their return capsules with parachutes. When a capsule reaches 8,500 metres above ground level, the parachutes open and slow it down, before it lands back on Earth with the astronauts inside. The safest landing spot is a large body of water, such as the ocean – this is called a "splashdown". The capsule is then gently loaded onto a boat, and the astronauts can get out. Then came something new – the Space Shuttle missions – and this is what Sally Ride trained for. Instead of a capsule, astronauts return to Earth by flying a Space Shuttle – which looks a bit like an aeroplane – and land on a specially built runway.

After training for a year, Sally was assigned the role of **mission specialist** for future shuttle missions. There was lots of interest in these missions from the media, but Sally didn't always get treated the same way as the men. Some news reporters didn't take her seriously and asked questions like:

"What if space affects your make-up?" and "Are you going to cry if something goes wrong?" None of the male astronaut candidates were asked those kinds of questions. She also refused the offer of a "space make-up kit" – the engineers had assumed it was something that she would want on the flight!

While she waited to go into space, Sally worked as a capsule communicator, or CAPCOM. This is someone on the ground who talks to the astronauts in space. Sally was the first female CAPCOM and carried out the job with accuracy and good humour. She also helped test, and was trained to use, a giant robotic arm known as the Canadarm. Testing was carried out on Earth, but on a space mission the Canadarm was attached to the Space Shuttle and operated by an astronaut. It was used for lots of different tasks including capturing satellites that needed to be repaired and assisting astronauts on spacewalks. It also had two cameras to film what life was like for the crew.

By now, Sally had all the experience needed to fly on the seventh Space Shuttle mission. On 18th June 1983, she was part of a five-person crew that launched into space on the Space Shuttle *Challenger*.

Sally was the first American woman in space, and at 32 years old, she was also the youngest American to go into space. Millions of people watched the launch on television and cheered her on.

While Sally was in space, she used the robotic arm to release satellites into orbit. She also conducted science experiments and helped with medical studies on her and her fellow astronauts. Sally's first flight lasted just over six days, and she said the view of Earth was spectacular. She also said: "It was the most fun I'll ever have in my life."

Astronauts are allowed to take personal items into space. This could be anything: books, a coffee machine and even musical instruments. On Sally's second spaceflight, a year after the first, she took a white silk scarf which had once belonged to the **pioneering** American pilot, Amelia Earhart. Two women, decades apart, who proved that there is a place for women in the air.

In total, Sally spent over 14 days in space – more than 343 hours across both missions. After she returned to Earth, NASA sent her on a tour of Europe. While she was in Hungary, Sally met the Russian cosmonaut, Svetlana Savitskaya, the second woman in space. The American astronauts had been instructed not to speak to any Russian cosmonauts, but Sally and Svetlana arranged a secret meeting where they talked for hours about spaceflight.

Sally continued to work at NASA, looking into space accidents – she investigated why they occurred and what NASA needed to do to prevent them. In 1986, when Space Shuttle *Challenger* exploded seconds after it had launched, Sally assisted with the investigation and used her expertise to make future missions safer.

She never went into space again, but Sally used her fame and knowledge to inspire others. "You can't be what you can't see," she used to say. That meant that if young girls didn't see women working as astronauts, scientists and engineers, they might think those roles weren't for them, or believe that they could do it too.

Sally became a Physics professor in 1989 and a **science communicator**. She wanted more young people to be inspired by science, as she'd been, and change the idea that science was "just for boys".

Along with her partner, Tam O'Shaughnessy, she set up Sally Ride Science, a company that created fun and interesting books, games and lessons to help children – especially girls – learn science in engaging ways. She never stopped visiting schools, giving talks and working with teachers. Sally also became an award-winning science writer for children; she and Tam co-wrote six children's books, including *Mission: Planet Earth* about climate change, and *To Space and Back*, about the human side of being an astronaut in space.

Sally died from cancer in 2012 aged 61, and she is remembered in many ways. In 2016, the US Navy named a research vessel after her – the *Sally Ride* sails across the globe to study the health of Earth's oceans.

In 2019, the toy and family entertainment company, Mattel, created a Sally Ride Barbie doll as part of its Inspiring Women collection and, in 2022, Sally was one of the first five women to have her face on one side of an American coin.

Sally wasn't only an inspiration; she was a leader. She reached for the stars and brought other people along for the ride too.

4. Dr Mae Jemison: First Black woman in space

In September 1966, when Mae Jemison was ten years old, a science fiction TV show called *Star Trek* burst onto TV screens. It was about a crew on a spaceship exploring strange new worlds throughout our galaxy. There had been other science fiction shows, but this one was different. It was the first time a Black actress in the US had been cast as a woman in authority: Lieutenant Uhura, played by Nichelle Nichols. Growing up, the only astronauts Mae Jemison would have seen were white men but now there was a Black woman shown working in space. Mae might not have realised it at the time, but that TV show had such an effect on her that she would go on to turn fictional entertainment into reality.

Mae loved science and astronomy from a young age, even before she'd seen *Star Trek*, and her parents told her she could do anything she set her mind to. She believed she could be an astronaut and kept dreaming and gazing at the stars. The Jemison family moved from Alabama to Chicago because Mae's parents thought it would give their children better educational opportunities – and it did.

Mae got such good grades at school she earned a scholarship to Stanford University when she was just 16 years old – that's two years earlier than most students! Mae studied Chemical Engineering and African and Afro-American Studies and while she did experience some racism while she was at university because, "Some professors would just pretend I wasn't there", this didn't stop Mae from wanting to succeed.

She became the head of the Black Student Union, **choreographed** a musical theatre show, learnt **Swahili** and took dance classes. She also studied hard. Mae might have found it difficult to decide what to specialise in – should she become a dancer or a doctor? – but she chose medicine and was accepted to Cornell Medical School in 1977. As part of her course, Mae led a medical study in Cuba, worked at a refugee camp in Thailand and then worked for the **Flying Doctors** in Kenya, East Africa. When she graduated, Mae practised as a doctor and signed up as a medical officer in the **Peace Corps**, working in Liberia and Sierra Leone, West Africa.

Mae always had her space dream in the back of her mind, and now there was an American female astronaut she could follow: Sally Ride. When Mae applied to NASA's astronaut programme in 1987, there were 2,000 people applying for 15 places. She was one of the 15 people selected, so what made her stand out from the others? The selectors at NASA were impressed with Mae's medical background. They could also see that she was determined and resilient – that's why she was successful.

The programme was tough – that hadn't changed! Scientific knowledge had moved on since Sally Ride had trained, but astronauts still needed to learn how to fly a jet, how to survive in emergency situations, and what it might be like to live in space.

But how do you train to do a spacewalk on Earth? First, you put on a spacesuit and then you're submerged in a giant, purpose-built swimming pool. This kind of underwater training helped Mae practise moving in the spacesuit and performing tasks while weightless. Astronauts have to train for seven hours in the pool for every hour they plan to spend on a spacewalk.

Mae trained to become a mission specialist so that she could conduct science experiments in space. On 12th September 1992, she was part of a seven-person crew that launched into space on the Space Shuttle *Endeavour*. She had made history as the first African American woman in space and, at the moment of launch, she quoted Lieutenant Uhura's famous line from *Star Trek*: "Hailing all frequencies open." Her childhood dream had come true!

Mae conducted lots of experiments on the effects of space motion sickness which is how the human body is affected by a microgravity environment. The crew also took some frogs and tadpoles with them, because it was thought that gravity would affect how they would grow in space. Mae thought it was "one of the coolest experiments ever" because the eggs developed just as if they were on Earth.

Astronauts were still allowed to take personal items into space, and Mae took a poster from her dance group, a West African **statuette** and a photo of Bessie Coleman, the first Black woman to get an international pilot's licence. Mae spent just over 190 hours in space, and showed the world that space is for everyone.

Mae chose to leave NASA in 1993, but she continued to do incredible things. She set up an international science camp for students aged 12 to 16 from under-represented backgrounds in STEM fields and who may face barriers to accessing STEM programmes. The camp, called The Earth We Share, is a place where children from all over the world come and stay for four weeks and learn team building, problem solving and science skills.

She has written many books for children and never forgotten her background in the arts. In 1993, Mae appeared in an episode of *Star Trek: The Next Generation*! She was also a technical consultant on the 2018 TV series *Mars*, and the cultural consultant on the 2022 Disney Pixar film *Lightyear*. LEGO created a Mae Jemison minifigure as part of their Women of NASA series. She continues to promote her belief that anyone can be a scientist, engineer, even an astronaut – it doesn't matter what you look like or where you come from. Mae once said, "Never limit yourself because of others' limited imagination"!

Despite being back on Earth, Mae still has her eyes firmly directed towards space. She leads the 100-Year Starship project, which aims to get humans to another star within the next 100 years. One of them could be you.

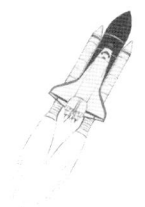

5. Dr Kalpana Chawla: First Indian woman in space

Kalpana Chawla was born in Karnal, India. On hot summer nights, the family would sleep on the flat roof of their house, where it was cooler. Kalpana would look up at the stars and the Moon and wonder if she would ever get to go to space and see it for herself.

The name "Kalpana" means "imagination" in Hindi, and she did have a big imagination. As a young girl, Kalpana liked drawing aeroplanes and she loved thinking about how birds and planes were able to fly. When aeroplanes flew overhead, she and her brother would ride their bicycles below them, trying to see where they were heading. She was always asking questions and wanting to know how things worked – this is what would set her on her first big journey across the world.

Kalpana did well at school. She liked Science, Maths and reading: her favourite books were about space, astronauts and flying. Kalpana knew that she could study anything, including subjects like space and astronomy. When she told her teachers that she wanted to fly a plane, they thought she was joking, but she wasn't. At that time in India, becoming a pilot or an engineer wasn't a traditional role for a girl but Kalpana's parents – particularly her mother – supported her goals.

Kalpana took Engineering classes and then studied Aeronautical Engineering – the study of how planes fly – before becoming the first woman to graduate with a degree in Aeronautical Engineering from Punjab Engineering College. Some of her teachers thought the aerospace industry wasn't for women and told her that she should study Electrical Engineering instead. Kalpana didn't listen, but she knew she had to make some big decisions. If she was going to succeed in aerospace engineering, she would need to go overseas to find the very best courses to study.

She moved to the US and studied at the University of Texas and then the University of Colorado, where she got her PhD in Aerospace Engineering. It wasn't easy for Kalpana because English wasn't her first language. She was a long way from her home and family, and there weren't many other women in her classes. But she never gave up.

Kalpana learnt how to fly small planes, got her pilot's licence and even started to teach flying. She didn't just fly from one location to another; she also flew aerobatics, which meant she could perform manoeuvres in a plane like loops, spins and rolls, which only very skilled pilots can perform.

In 1988, Kalpana started working for NASA at the Ames Research Center, where her job involved looking at simulations of air flow around aircraft.

What she really wanted was to join the NASA astronaut programme. In 1994, she became a US citizen, she was accepted onto the astronaut programme and in 1995 her training finally began.

As part of her training, Kalpana learnt to drive an armoured personnel carrier (APC).

These are military vehicles used to transport soldiers safely across battlefields and they're designed to withstand an explosion from a landmine or **enemy fire**. Why would astronauts need to drive vehicles like this? It was all about safety. If anything went wrong before the rocket boosters ignited during a shuttle launch, the astronauts would evacuate the shuttle quickly and drive away from the launchpad in the APC. The vehicles were modified to be heat resistant, and have their own oxygen system to keep the astronauts safe from a shuttle fire or a fuel leak while they made their getaway.

As part of this emergency evacuation safety training, Kalpana also needed to practise using a zip wire. That might sound a bit odd but, at the time Kalpana was training, the quickest way from a space shuttle to the ground was by using a zip wire. This wasn't a zip wire like the ones you might find at a playground or park. This mega zip wire was over 400 metres long. That's the length of about 48 buses lined up end-to-end.

Kalpana was chosen for her first space mission, becoming part of the crew on the Space Shuttle *Columbia*, which launched in 1997. As a mission specialist, Kalpana was in charge of operating the robotic arm, like the one Sally Ride used, and she was also the **backup engineer**. It was during this flight that Kalpana made history as the first Indian woman to go into space. She even received a phone call from the Prime Minister of India, Inder Kumar Gujral, while she was up there. He told her that this was a moment of national pride, and he wanted the crew to visit India on their return.

Kalpana spent 15 days and 16 hours on that first flight, flying 10.5 million kilometres in 252 orbits of Earth. She used the robotic arm to launch a satellite and completed lots of experiments in microgravity, including looking at how flames burn in space. When she wasn't working, Kalpana enjoyed looking out of the window at Earth below and said, "When you look at the stars and the galaxy, you feel that you are not just from one piece of land, but from the Solar System."

When she got back to Earth, Kalpana led the Astronaut Corps Crew Systems and Habitability department. This department focuses on the practical side of living and working in space: what kind of equipment astronauts might need to use, mission-specific training and understanding the layout of the spacecraft habitat and how it's used by the astronauts on board.

In January 2003, Kalpana went on a second mission, also on *Columbia*, which had been updated and modified since Kalpana's first flight. She carried out over 80 science experiments during her 16 days in space, looking at how this environment affects humans, plants and even fire. The crew worked in shifts so that experiments could take place all the time: the Red team worked while the Blue team slept, and then they switched around. Kalpana was in the Red team. She loved it! She sent messages back to Earth to tell everyone how much fun she was having, how exciting it was and how lucky she felt. In her last message from space she said, "The path from dreams to success does exist. May you have the vision to find it, the courage to get onto it, and the perseverance to follow it."

On 1st February 2003, as *Columbia* was returning to Earth, there was a problem. What the astronauts didn't know was that a piece of foam insulation had broken off and damaged part of the craft during its launch. This damage caused one of the wings to melt and the shuttle exploded as it re-entered Earth's atmosphere. All seven members of the crew died, including Kalpana. After this tragic accident, NASA stopped all spaceflights for two years while more safety checks were introduced.

Kalpana's name, and those of all the astronauts on *Columbia*, live on. A building at the Punjab Engineering College, where Kalpana had studied, was named after her and a prize fund was created in her honour to reward the top students in the Aeronautical Engineering department. The KALPANA-1 satellite was named after her; books and TV shows have told her story to millions. Kalpana had an asteroid, a lunar crater and a peak on Mars named after her, and a supply capsule sent to the ISS was named the S.S. Kalpana Chawla. She was awarded the Congressional Space Medal of Honor by US President George Bush, and the Government of Karnataka in India created the Kalpana Chawla Award to recognise young women scientists.

Kalpana once said, "You must enjoy the journey because whether or not you get there, you must have fun on the way." Maybe the next time you look up at the night sky, remember Kalpana – the girl from India who reached for the stars … and became one.

6. Helen Sharman: Britain's first astronaut

If you like chocolate, you'll love the role Helen Sharman had at the sweet company, Mars. Helen was a chemist there, and part of her job was to take samples of chocolate from the production line and taste them. She hadn't ever thought about becoming an astronaut, but as Helen was driving home from work one day, she heard an unusual advert on the radio: "Astronaut wanted, no experience necessary". The advert was for Project Juno, a private space programme hoping to send the first British person into space. It was a partnership between Russia and the UK, with the aim of strengthening the relationship between the two nations. The successful applicant would be sent to work on the Russian Mir Space Station and conduct experiments in space.

By the time Helen got home, she had decided to apply. Although the advert said applicants didn't need any experience, she did have some useful interests and qualifications. At school in Sheffield, Helen took A-level Chemistry and Physics, where she was the only girl in her classes. Encouraged by her parents, Helen's interest in science grew and she went on to study Chemistry at university, followed by a PhD. Helen had always loved learning languages and sports as well as science – here was the opportunity to combine all these things.

The experts running the programme wanted someone who was trustworthy and could work well with other people. The right person needed to be physically fit, with a background in science and the ability to learn Russian. Helen filled out the application form, and she was invited to interviews, where she was given problem-solving tests and logic puzzles to complete. She also underwent medical checks and fitness training. About 13,000 people applied to that radio advert, but only one was eventually chosen to go into space: Helen!

For 18 months, Helen trained alongside Russian cosmonauts at Star City, which is a special training ground for astronauts, just outside Moscow, Russia. She studied advanced mechanics and, like the astronauts who had come before her, learnt what to do in an emergency and how to live, eat and sleep in a microgravity environment. Her favourite training exercise was going on a parabolic flight to simulate weightlessness.

On 18th May 1991, Helen and two Russian cosmonauts launched into space on the Soyuz TM-12 spacecraft and headed for the Mir Space Station.

Helen remembered everything she'd been taught as she felt the G-force during launch pushing her into her chair. There was a science laboratory on the space station and Helen carried out experiments to learn how the different atmosphere and weightlessness affected a plant's growth.

Mir Space Station in orbit above Earth.

Helen's cargo included wheat seeds, potato roots and a lemon tree. She also took photos of the UK from space and answered questions from children on Earth via radio. Imagine being in school and chatting to an astronaut in orbit!

Living in space was fun but unusual – there wasn't a shower like the one you might have in your bathroom. Helen had to use rinse-less soap and shampoo with a face cloth and a small amount of water from a pouch. She described it as a "sponge bath". Her favourite part of the experience was the feeling of weightlessness, and she said it's "something that I still dream about. It feels natural, free and relaxing." She also claimed that "sleeping on the wall or the ceiling is an entirely reasonable thing to do in space!"

Like other astronauts before her, Helen took along some personal belongings: a photo of Queen Elizabeth II, and a butterfly brooch that her dad had given her. Helen also took an identification document, which she called a "space passport", so that she could be identified if she landed in a different country when they came back home.

Eight days after launch, Helen returned to Earth. Russian capsules now used different technology, and Helen didn't have to jump out with a parachute like Valentina Tereshkova. Like the US capsules before the Space Shuttle programme, it had parachutes. The seats in the capsule were specially built to absorb the impact of a bumpy landing and **retro-rockets** fired just before landing to help reduce speed even more.

It wasn't a splashdown in the ocean for Helen – the Russian capsules were designed to touch down on land – so she had a safe, if bumpy, landing in Kazakhstan. At the age of 27, she was officially Britain's first astronaut!

Helen never went on another space mission, even though she did say that she would have liked to have gone on a spacewalk. She wrote books about her experiences and talked about space in schools, on TV and radio and at special events. She was a presenter on the TV shows *Stargazing Live* and *The Sky at Night*, and said, "I love how science explains the whole world around us."

The Soyuz capsule returning to Earth.

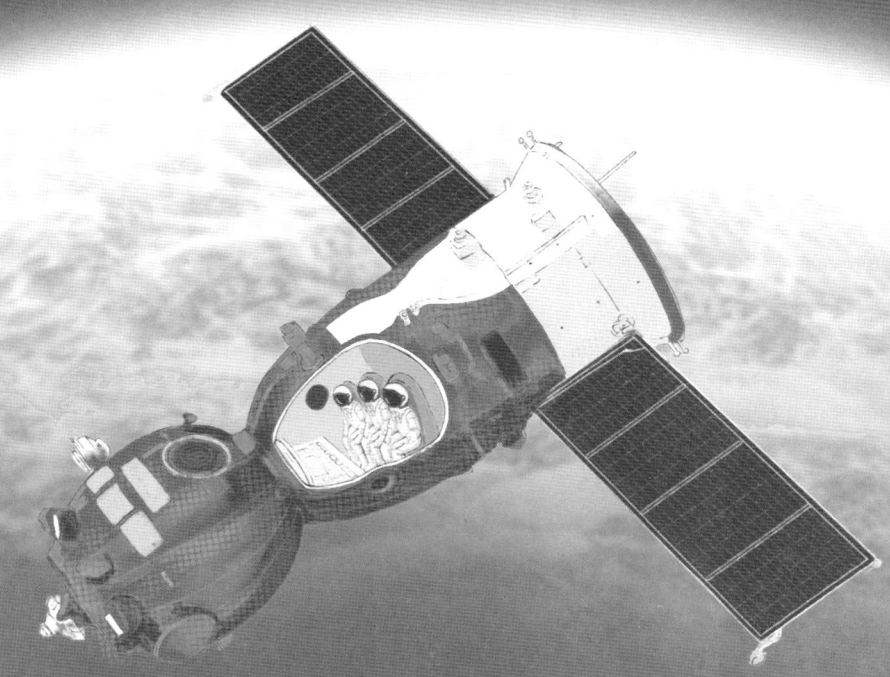

Helen continues to champion the importance of STEM subjects and has received many awards for her work, including a star on the **Sheffield Walk of Fame**, an **OBE** and a **CMG**.

People often ask Helen if she believes in aliens. She replies in the same way. There are billions of stars and numerous planets, so it's likely there are other life forms elsewhere in the universe. In *this* small part of the universe, Helen's journey from Sheffield to space shows us that anyone can do anything, and you never know what opportunities are around the corner. Say yes to things and have a go, work hard, believe in yourself and you might make history. As Helen said: "Science opens up the world – it's such an interesting topic and it enables you to play a part in discovery and making our world better."

7. Anuradha T.K.: First female space director

Anuradha T.K. wasn't an astronaut, but she was a trailblazer in the space industry. She grew up in **Bangalore** which was, and still is, a global hub for science and technology. Like all the amazing women we've met so far, Anuradha T.K. was an inquisitive child. She loved finding out how things worked and says she would ask her parents how stars shone, and why the Moon changed shape across the month.

At school, she loved Maths and Science, particularly number puzzles and space science. Anuradha T.K. also enjoyed reading, especially about rockets, stars and planets. In 1969, when she was nine years old, Neil Armstrong walked on the Moon.

Anuradha T.K. didn't watch the television footage, because her family didn't have a TV, but she did hear about it from her teachers. The news about the Apollo 11 landing "really ignited [her] imagination".

In India at that time, it wasn't usual for girls to work in the space industry, but that's *exactly* what Anuradha T.K. wanted to do, and no one was going to stop her. She studied Electronics and Communication Engineering at the University Visvesvaraya College of Engineering in Bangalore.

After graduating, her first job was working for the Indian Space Research Organisation (ISRO). Anuradha T.K.'s qualifications made her the perfect choice, and she tested satellites at the Satellite Centre in Bangalore. She soon noticed that there weren't many women in the labs or the control rooms. In fact, at that time, there were only six women working for ISRO, but she didn't find that a problem. "You don't get any special treatment because you're a woman," she said. "You're also not discriminated against because you're a woman. You're treated as an equal here."

Anuradha T.K. with the rocket used to launch satellites into space.

At ISRO, Anuradha T.K. had to check that satellites remained in the right place in space. Even if a satellite moves just a little bit left or right, it could stop working or affect how well it does its job.

Satellites are used for communication (TV, internet, smartphones), predicting and monitoring the weather, and as navigation tools and to study space, so they need to be built and maintained to work as efficiently as possible. This meant that Anuradha T.K.'s job was important. She had to make careful, precise calculations, and she needed to be able to think fast.

Anuradha T.K. became an expert in satellite communications – helping satellites "talk" to Earth and send information back and forth. She created a new way to successfully move a type of satellite called "geosynchronous satellites" (GSAT). These satellites move at the same speed as Earth, so they can remain positioned over a specific place on Earth as it rotates.

Anuradha T.K. led the first all-women research team and used her methods to get an Indian communication satellite, called GSAT-12, into orbit from Satish Dhawan Space Centre, Sriharikota, India. It was her work that made GSAT-12 a success.

GSAT-12 in orbit

In 2012, Anuradha T.K. was promoted to **project director** in charge of launching more communication satellites. She led a team and was responsible for making sure every launch went according to plan. Without the GSAT communication satellites, people in small, remote villages in India would have no way to get in contact with others, so Anuradha's work provided important services. She also helped launch the Indian National Satellite System (INSAT) satellites, which meant people could receive TV programmes, internet services and weather forecasting information.

Anuradha T.K. showed everyone what an effective leader a female space scientist could be. Women could handle the pressure of space missions and navigate big responsibilities. She said, "We don't need to shout to be heard. Our work speaks for itself."

She has inspired her family too – one of Anuradha T.K.'s daughters is a computer science engineer and another is studying to be an electronics engineer. She believes that if young people see what many women in the space industry have achieved, they might think, "If she can do it, so can I." Anuradha T.K. gives talks in schools and universities and she encourages young people to enjoy Science and Maths, just as she does. She tells women and girls that they don't have to pick between a family or a career. "Once girls see that there are lots of women in the space program, they get motivated."

Anuradha T.K. became the first woman to be a satellite project director at ISRO and won many awards in recognition of her work. She stayed at ISRO for 34 years and is the most senior woman to have worked there. She's retired now, but keeps inspiring people by giving lectures. Her knowledge and passion gave her the determination to succeed. She's shown children that it's OK to ask questions, and it's OK to dream.

8. Spacesuit seamstresses

The 1969 Apollo 11 mission was the first time that humans walked on solid ground which wasn't Earth. But it wasn't just about the men who stood on the Moon, there was a whole team of people supporting them, including the women who sewed for this Apollo mission!

Spacesuits were worn by astronauts before the Apollo missions, but this one was different. For the first time, astronauts would be expected to move around outside the spacecraft and not remain inside a capsule, so a different kind of suit was needed. These spacesuits had to act as a mini spacecraft for each of the astronauts – to keep them at the right temperature and protect them from **radiation** and **micrometeorite** strikes. They would provide air to breathe and room to move around, work outside the spacecraft and explore the Moon's surface. Without their spacesuits, the astronauts wouldn't survive.

These spacesuits weren't made by space scientists or engineers and, at that time, there were no robots or giant machines to help out. They were hand sewn by a team of **seamstresses**, using regular sewing machines that people used at home.

The women worked in the Special Products Division at a company called International Latex Corporation (ILC), in Delaware, US. Latex is a material made from rubber, and it's used in the manufacture of gloves worn to provide protection against infection. Latex can be durable and flexible and made to be very thin. The strong but lightweight and flexible material that ILC worked with could be used to create something perfect for spacesuits too.

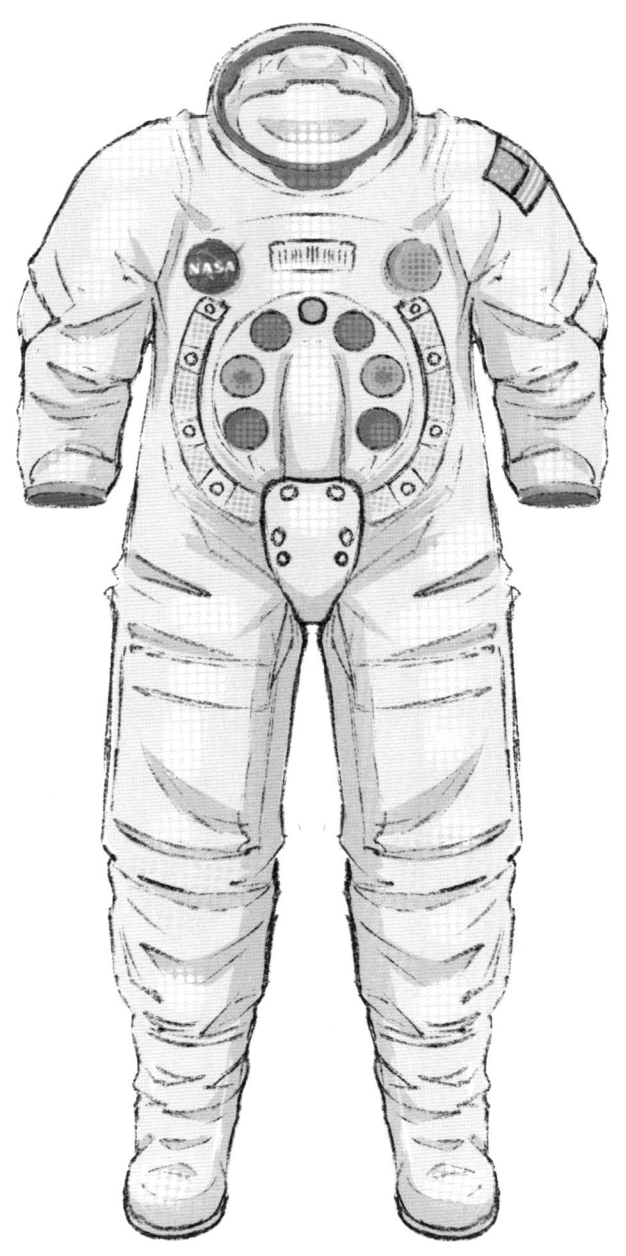

ILC had created a flexible, new material which combined webbing, latex and nylon straps. They came up with a design proposal for the spacesuits that included using this new material at the joints of the suit, making it similar to the design of a bendable drinking straw. NASA agreed that ILC would work with an engineering company called Hamilton Standard: the team at ILC would design and manufacture the spacesuits using their revolutionary material, and Hamilton Standard would design and make the backpack, which supplied the astronauts with oxygen.

There were many skilled women making the suits: seamstresses, **pattern cutters** and assemblers, many of whom were working-class African Americans. Every one of them played an important role in the design and construction of the spacesuits worn by all 12 men who went to the Moon. They were trained to work with engineers on how to read blueprints, which were the specially drawn designs and layouts for the spacesuits. The material they were working with was so expensive, it was kept in a safe!

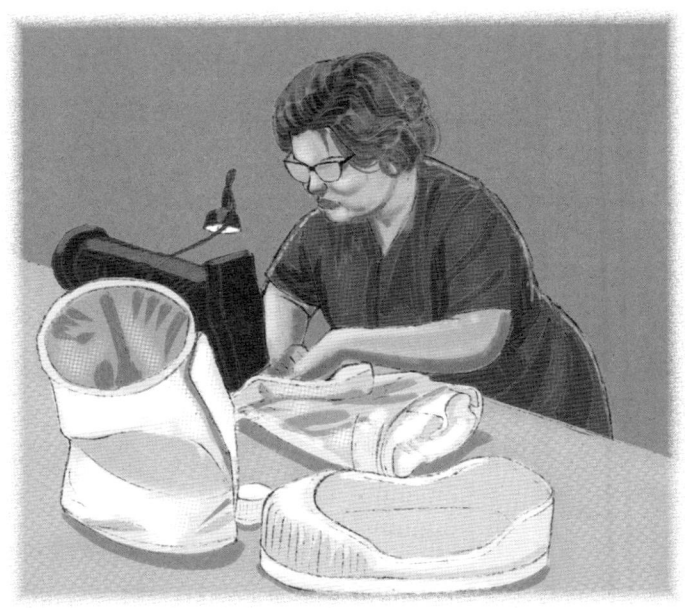

These super stitchers had steady hands and skills that were out of this world. They often worked with tricky materials under huge time pressures, and they knew the importance of each stitch to make the garments exactly right. One incorrect stitch on a spacesuit might cause the suit to leak precious air or burst open; it was incredibly important work.

Eleanor Foraker led a team that was given the important task of sewing each Apollo suit by hand. Each suit had 21 layers of material, and each layer had a different, equally important, role. Some material blocked radiation, some protected the wearer from heat, some had the ability to keep sweat away from the body, some absorbed fluid, and some trapped air. The astronauts had to fit into the bulky suits with the minimum amount of difficulty, and bend, walk, climb and move. Some layers were stretchy, others were stiff, and they all had to fit perfectly. Even normal processes, like pinning the layers together, needed additional thought – if you used too many pins, the material would have too many holes in it, which could also be dangerous in space. The sewing machines were run incredibly slowly for accuracy, and some of the layers were glued together one piece at a time.

Eleanor devised a clever way of making sure no pins were lost in the garments. She gave everyone their own set of coloured pins; at the end of the shift, each woman had to account for all of them. Because they each had their own colours, there was never any doubt about who had left a pin stuck in a spacesuit, or where it might be! Some women sewed the main body of the suit, some made the gloves, boots, helmets or other sections. Each part had to be perfect and work seamlessly with the other pieces.

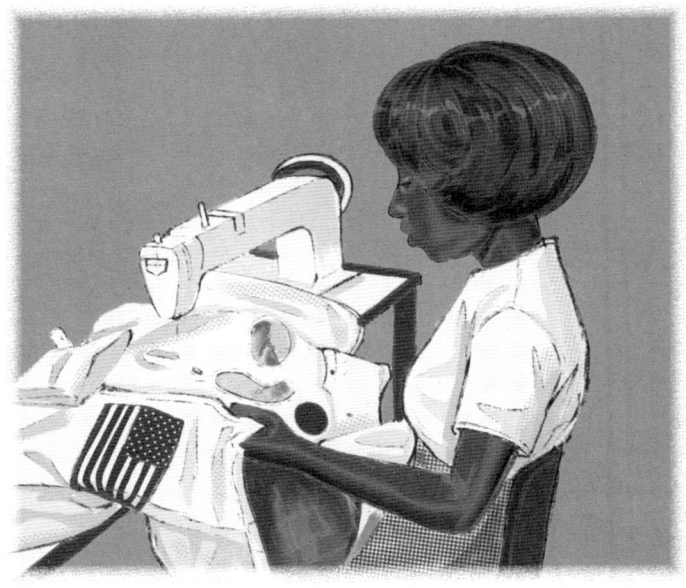

Once the suits were sewn, they were tested. They were filled with air to mimic the shape of a human inside, then stretched, bent, twisted, heated, cooled and thrown around to check that they wouldn't tear. If one single thread broke or came loose, the suit went back to the sewing machine. The finished suits were also X-rayed at a local hospital to ensure there were no pins left in them. This process was repeated until everything was ready.

When Neil Armstrong took his famous step and leap for humankind and walked on the Moon, the suit fitted and worked perfectly. Armstrong was able to move safely and easily, and looked fantastic! Buzz Aldrin was the second man on the Moon and his suit also worked just as well. Every tiny stitch and perfect fold, crease and seam, sewn by Eleanor and her team, kept each astronaut alive.

Iona Allen constructed Neil Armstrong's lunar boots – imagine seeing the first man on the Moon and knowing you had made those boots! In 1972, one of the team – Roberta Pilkenton – had to make an emergency repair to a spacesuit so that the Apollo 17 mission could launch on time. Roberta was sent to Florida with the materials in a briefcase which was handcuffed to her wrist, so she didn't lose it. She'd never been on a plane before, but she flew to Florida, got to the Kennedy Space Centre at 4:00 a.m., and worked for 20 hours to repair a leg joint on the spacesuit.

The names of the seamstresses who made the spacesuits and kept those astronauts alive weren't known or celebrated at the time. They didn't become famous for their work, but they were all heroes. Eleanor Foraker said, "It was exciting and challenging and we were so proud." The team didn't work hard because they wanted recognition, but because they knew how important their work was going to be.

Joanne Thompson said, "We knew a man's life was going to depend on it, so we just kept on going."

The sewers didn't just sew for the Apollo missions – they made suits for astronauts on other missions too. Even today, some parts of the spacesuits are handsewn by people at ILC. Nowadays, the suits are lighter and more flexible, and they are made from some different materials, but they still have to be perfectly sewn, and the teamwork and skill is the same. If you see an Apollo suit in a museum, look closely at the tiny stitches and think about the team behind them.

You don't have to be an astronomer or an engineer to work in the space industry, and you might not become famous. But everything matters, and everyone works together, to get people into space. From the tiniest stitches to the biggest rockets, everyone has a part to play. Remember that next time you see TV footage of an astronaut in space!

9. The future!

The space industry has changed so much in the last 50 years. What's going to happen in the decades ahead? Jobs in the space industry may change – there will be new roles, some of which haven't even been invented yet.

We'll still need astronauts, astronomers, engineers and scientists, but new jobs will emerge as we travel to new places and discover new things.

We may need space architects to design habitats on the Moon and Mars, and on worlds we haven't discovered yet, and space builders to construct them.

We'll need astrobiologists to search further and deeper for signs of life in our universe. You could be a robotics engineer, Artificial Intelligence (AI) specialist or computer programmer, designing and building machines to work in new environments. You might be a space farmer, growing food in space or on other planets, or maybe even a space tour guide showing people around the solar system. What about being a space politician or a lawyer, deciding how things are done on other planets?

Technicians could work on important climate change projects, coding space satellites and analysing data. Or maybe they could design and create the newest space garments for interplanetary travel. More people may live and work on new space stations for months at a time, even years, like astronauts currently on the ISS. We don't know what might be achievable in the next 50 or 100 years. These could be the dream jobs of the future. One thing is certain: the possibilities are as vast as space itself, because we know the future isn't just shaped by new technology and industry, but by people.

So, what will *your* starry story be? Will you build the ships that carry us away from Earth to faraway moons and planets teeming with life? Will you be the one who teaches the next generation about stars and the universe? Or will you inspire others by following your own path? The future is continually being written, and the space industry is changing every day. You have the power to help shape it yourself. Space needs minds just like yours.

So, keep wondering, keep learning, keep asking questions. With space, the sky isn't the limit of what you might achieve, it's just the beginning.

Glossary

backup engineer fully trained engineer who can take over mission operations, testing or launch responsibilities if the main engineer isn't available

Bangalore modern-day Bengaluru

centrifuge a machine that spins very fast – used to train astronauts

choreographed created a sequence of steps or moves

CMG stands for Companion of the Order of St Michael and St George, an honour awarded to individuals who served the country

decompression chambers small rooms where you can change the air pressure

enemy fire gunfire from an opposing side in a conflict

extraterrestrial something that comes from outside Earth

Flying Doctors a service that provides essential medical services, particularly to remote areas, via air transport

ground control the team within mission control that makes sure messages and data travel safely between Earth and the spacecraft

microgravity weak gravity, so that people or objects appear to be weightless

micrometeorite small pieces of rock or metal from comets or asteroids

mission control a team of people on Earth who monitor a spacecraft from launch to landing. It is also the name of the building where the team work.

mission specialist an astronaut who performs special jobs like experiments or fixing equipment

OBE stands for Order of the British Empire, an honour awarded to people who have made a significant contribution in areas such as the arts, sciences and charity work

pattern cutters professionals who create templates for clothes

Peace Corps an independent US government agency that sends volunteers abroad to help community development and promote peace

pioneering someone who has achieved something for the first time by using new ideas or methods

primitive basic

project director an experienced scientist or engineer who runs a space project from start to finish

radiation waves of energy, heat or particles from an object that can sometimes be harmful

retro-rockets small rocket engines that slow down how fast a vehicle is moving

science communicator someone who explains science in a clear way so everyone can understand it

seamstresses women who sew

Sheffield Walk of Fame also called Sheffield Legends, an area celebrating famous people from, or connected to, Sheffield, UK

Soviet Union the name given to a group of regions that Russia was a part of at that time

space tourists people who travel to space for pleasure rather than research or work

statuette a small statue

Swahili language used in the East Africa and Congo region

videographers people who make video films

Book talk questions

Do you believe we are alone in the universe? Why or why not?

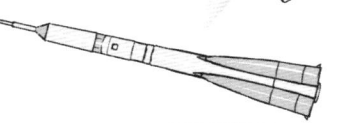

Why is it important to study space?

What roles can someone do to be involved in space research?

Which of the women in this book was your favourite, and why?

What is the first thing you would do in space if you were an astronaut?

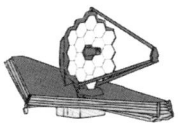

Which part of being an astronaut do you think is the most challenging?

What would you like to find out about space?

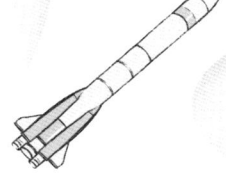

What part of this book inspired you the most?

How do the women in the book serve as role models for girls interested in science and space?

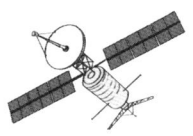

What are your dreams for the future?

Ask the author

Have you met any of the women in this book?
I have met, and know, Helen Sharman. We first met at an event for a space education charity we both supported and we got to know each other then.

What inspired you to write a book about women in the space industry?
I am a woman in the space industry! I feel like we've got books about male astronauts and maybe know a little about some of the women, but I've not really seen a book just about women in the space industry, so I wanted to write one.

How did you go about researching the stories of these women? What surprised you the most?
I read magazine articles, webpages, books and interviews, and I noticed a pattern. All the women were naturally curious as children, and they all had to work a little bit harder than their male counterparts to get to where they wanted to be.

What is your favourite book about space?
I like the children's book *Here We Are* by Oliver Jeffers.

What big question about space exploration would you like to be answered the most?
I want to know if aliens exist!

Why is it important to have diverse voices and perspectives in the space industry?
It is important in any industry, because diverse voices and perspectives bring so much! Having diverse voices in the space industry is important because it brings fresh ideas, fairer opportunities, stronger teamwork, and decisions that better reflect and benefit all of humanity. We all live on the same planet, under the same sky, so we should work together to celebrate that.

What can young readers do next to stay curious about space exploration?
Read! Reading is a great way to transport you to other worlds and for you to stay curious. You don't need any special equipment to be a scientist or an astronomer. You just need to go outside and look up!

Published by Collins
An imprint of HarperCollins*Publishers*

The News Building
1 London Bridge Street
London SE1 9GF
UK

Macken House
39/40 Mayor Street Upper
Dublin 1
D01 C9W8
Ireland

Text © Dr Sheila Kanani 2026
Design and illustrations © HarperCollins*Publishers* Limited 2026

10 9 8 7 6 5 4 3 2 1

ISBN 9780008784751

All rights reserved. No part of this publication may be reproduced, stored in a retrieval system, or transmitted in any form by any means, electronic, mechanical, photocopying, recording or otherwise, without the prior written permission of the Publisher or a licence permitting restricted copying in the United Kingdom issued by the Copyright Licensing Agency Ltd, 5th Floor, Shackleton House, 4 Battle Bridge Lane, London SE1 2HX.

Without limiting the exclusive rights of any author, contributor or the publisher of this publication, any unauthorised use of this publication to train generative artificial intelligence (AI) technologies is expressly prohibited. HarperCollins also exercise their rights under Article 4(3) of the Digital Single Market Directive 2019/790 and expressly reserve this publication from the text and data mining exception.

British Library Cataloguing-in-Publication Data
A catalogue record for this publication is available from the British Library.

Author: Dr Sheila Kanani
Illustrator: Fifa Adoglo (Illo Agency)
Publisher: Laura White
Commissioning editor: Holly Woolnough
Development editor: Zoë Clarke
Product manager: Holly Woolnough
Content editor: Selin Akca
Copyeditor: Sally Byford

Proofreader: Sasha Morton
Reviewer: Lisa Davis
Fact checker: Sasha Morton
Cover designer: Sarah Finan
Internal designer: 2Hoots Publishing Services Ltd
Typesetter: David Jimenez
Production controller: Sophie Waeland

Collins would like to thank the teachers and children at Grange Primary School, Southwark, for being part of the development of Big Cat Read On.

Printed in the UK

 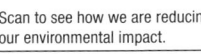

Made with responsibly sourced paper and vegetable ink

Scan to see how we are reducing our environmental impact.

Get the latest Collins Big Cat news at
collins.co.uk/collinsbigcat

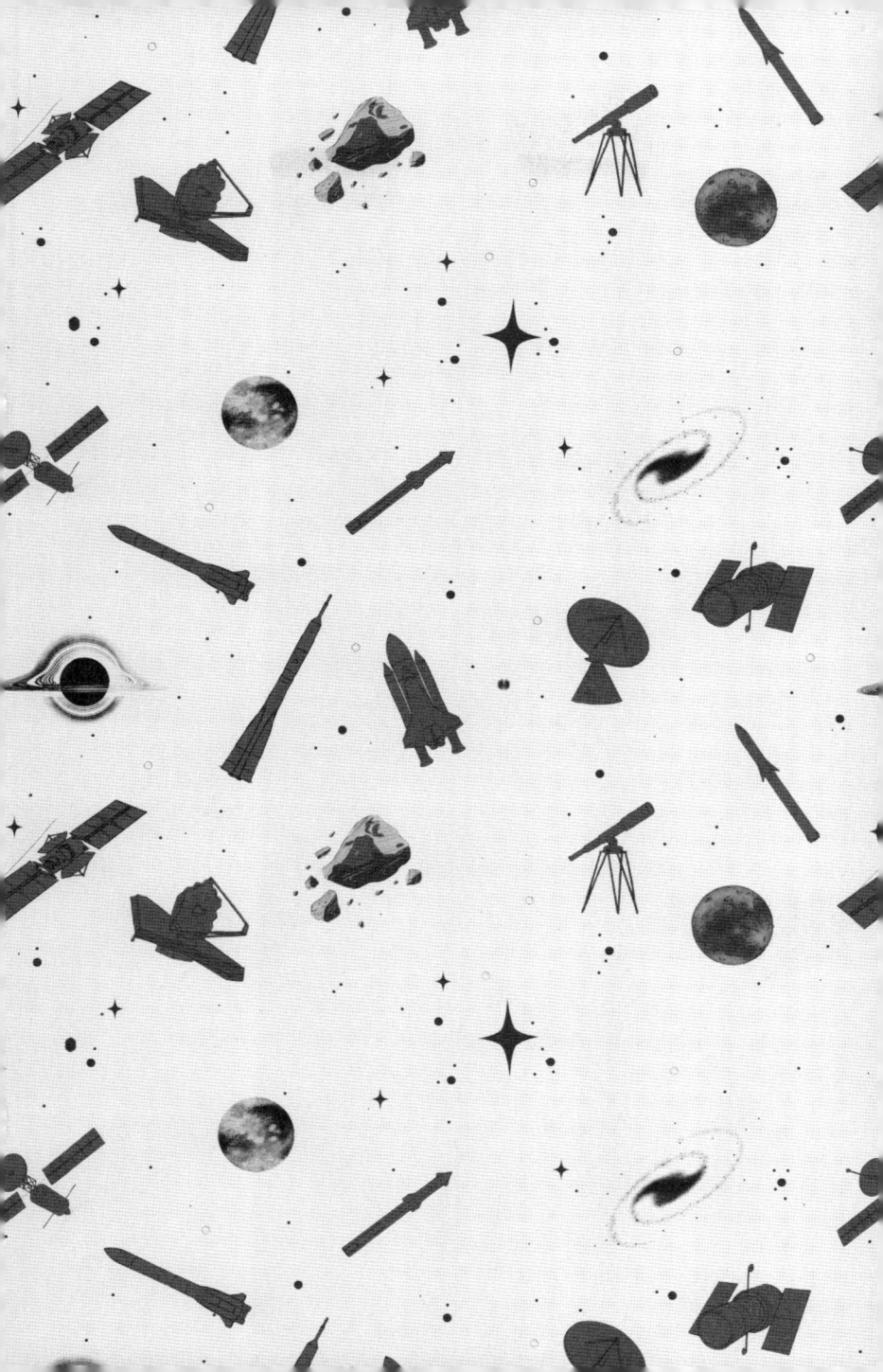

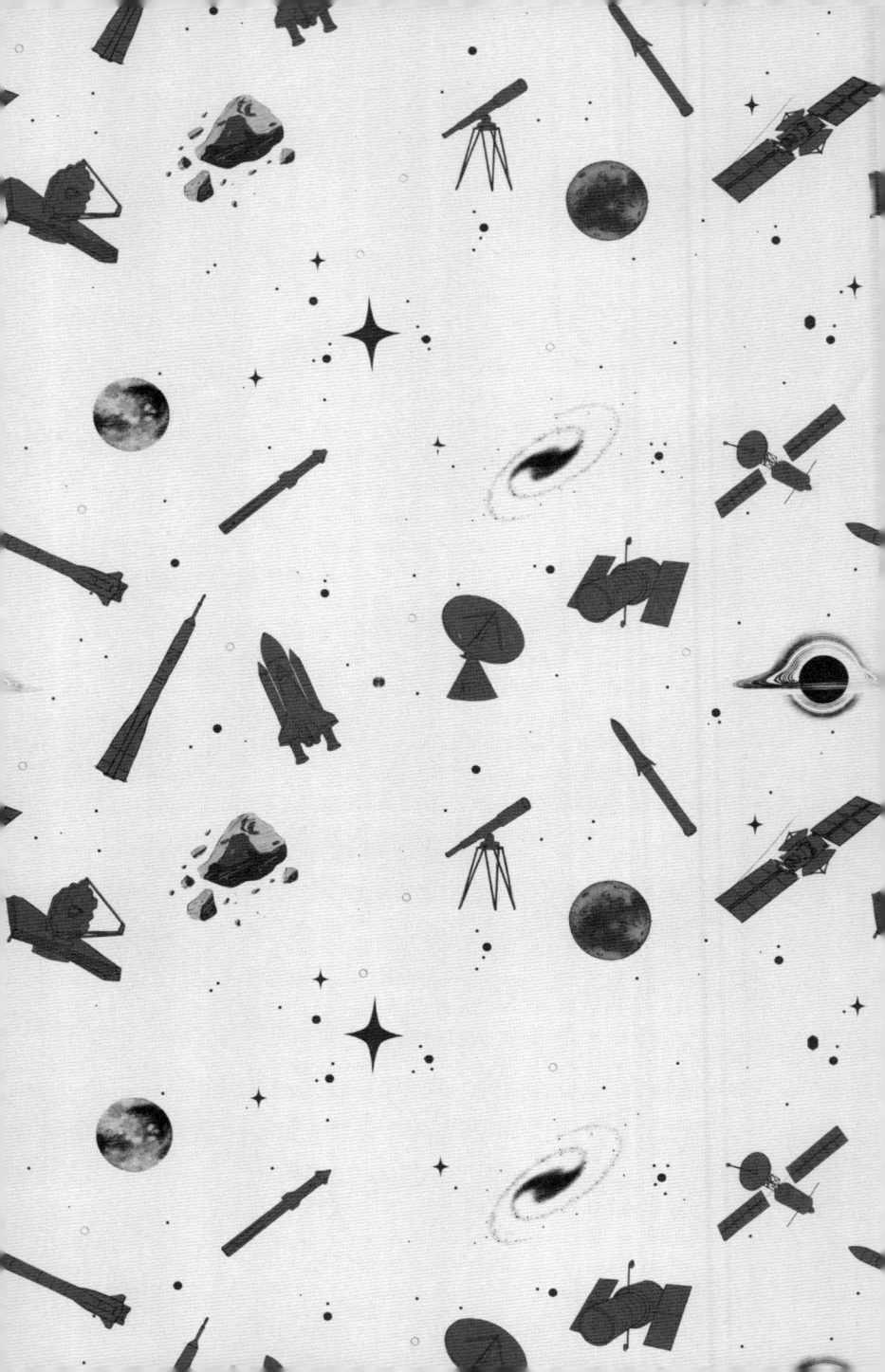